Denise Levertov, whose mother is Welsh and whose father, an Anglican clergyman, was by birth a Russian Jew, was born in 1923 in London and grew up in suburban Ilford, Essex. She was educated at home (never attending school or college), studied ballet for a time, and worked as a nurse during the war. Married to the writer Mitchell Goodman in 1947, she came to the United States the following year. Their son Nikolai was born in 1949.

Miss Levertov has read her poems at many colleges, as well as the Poetry Centers of New York and San Francisco. During 1961 and again from 1963 through 1965 she served as Poetry Editor of *The Nation*. She has taught at Drew University, C.C.N.Y., the Poetry Center (YMHA, New York), and Vassar College. She has been a Guggenheim Fellow, a Scholar of the Radcliffe Institute for Independent Study, and the recipient of a National Institute of Arts and Letters grant.

The poet's first book, *The Double Image*, was published by the Cresset Press, London, in 1946. Her first American publication was in *The New British Poets*, an anthology edited by Kenneth Rexroth, published in 1948 by New Directions. Since then, she has been considered an American poet and has published *Here and Now* (City Lights, 1957), *Overland to the Islands* (Jargon Books, 1958), *With Eyes at the Back of Our Heads* (New Directions, 1960), *The Jacob's Ladder* (New Directions, 1961), *O Taste and See* (New Directions, 1964), and *The Sorrow Dance* (New Directions, 1967).

THE SORROW DANCE

Other Books by Denise Levertov

The Double Image

Here and Now

Overland to the Islands

With Eyes at the Back of Our Heads

The Jacob's Ladder

O Taste and See

Denise Levertov

The Sorrow Dance

New Directions

Acknowledgments

Some of these poems first appeared in the following magazines, to whose editors grateful acknowledgment is made by author and publisher: *Agenda* (London), *Angel Hair, Arts & Sciences, Arts & Society, Brown Paper, The Chicago Review, Fubbalo, Hanging Loose, The Harvard Advocate, Love, Magazine, The Nation, Nation Centennial, The New England Galaxy, North American Review, Occidental Review, Open Places, The Paris Review, Peace News* (London), *Quarterly Review of Literature, Sisters Today, Some/thing, Sum, Synapse, Syracuse 10, Things, University of Tampa Poetry Review, Upriver.* "City Psalm" first appeared as a broadsheet in the Oyez series, Berkeley, California. "Psalm Concerning the Castle" first appeared as a broadsheet published by Walter Hamady, Detroit, Michigan. The following poems first appeared in *Poetry* (Chicago): "Olga Poems," "Life at War," "A Vision."

The author wishes to thank the Radcliffe Institute for Independent Study and the National Institute of Arts and Letters for their help during the period many of these poems were written.

The quotation from Louis MacNeice in "Olga Poems" is from his *Solstices.* © 1961 by Louis MacNeice. Reprinted by courtesy of Oxford University Press, Inc.

The quotation from Rainer Maria Rilke in "Life at War" is from *Letters of Rainer Maria Rilke,* Volume Two, 1910–1926. Translated by Jane Bannard Greene and M. D. Herter Norton. Copyright 1947, 1948 by W. W. Norton & Company, Inc., New York, N. Y. Reprinted by permission from the publisher.

The quotation from Rilke in "Joy" is from *Selected Letters of Rilke* translated by R. F. C. Hull, reprinted by permission of the publishers, Macmillan and Co. Ltd.

Manufactured in the United States of America.

New Directions Books are published for James Laughlin by New Directions Publishing Corporation, 333 Sixth Avenue, New York 10014.

Dedicated to
Harry Green
in memory of Olga
and to
Betty Kray

Contents

Something hangs in back of me,
I can't see it, can't move it.

I know it's black,
a hump on my back.

It's heavy. You
can't see it.

What's in it? Don't tell me
you don't know. It's

what you told me about—
black

inimical power, cold
whirling out of it and

around me and
sweeping you flat.

But what if,
like a camel, it's

pure energy I store,
and carry humped and heavy?

Not black, not
that terror, stupidity

of cold rage; or black
only for being pent there?

What if released in air
it became a white

source of light, a fountain
of light? Could all that weight

be the power of flight?
Look inward: see me

with embryo wings, one
feathered in soot, the other

blazing ciliations of ember, pale
flare-pinions. Well—

could I go
on one wing,

the white one?

Woman fears for man, he goes
out alone to his labors. No mirror
nests in his pocket. His face
opens and shuts with his hopes.
His sex hangs unhidden
or rises before him
blind and questing.

She thinks herself
lucky. But sad. When she goes out
she looks in the glass, she remembers
herself. Stones, coal,
the hiss of water upon the kindled
branches—her being
is a cave, there are bones at the hearth.

A nervous smile as gaze meets
gaze across
deep
river.
What place
for a smile here;
        it edges away

leaves us each at ravine's edge
alone with our bodies.

We plunge—
O dark river!
towards each other—
into that element—

a deep fall,
the eyes closing as if forever,
the air ripping, the waters
cleaving and closing upon us.

Heavy we are, our flesh
of stone and velvet goes down,
goes down.

What is green in me
darkens, muscadine.

If woman is inconstant,
good, I am faithful to

ebb and flow, I fall
in season and now

is a time of ripening.
If her part

is to be true,
a north star,

good, I hold steady
in the black sky

and vanish by day,
yet burn there

in blue or above
quilts of cloud.

There is no savor
more sweet, more salt

than to be glad to be
what, woman,

and who, myself,
I am, a shadow

that grows longer as the sun
moves, drawn out

on a thread of wonder.
If I bear burdens

they begin to be remembered
as gifts, goods, a basket

of bread that hurts
my shoulders but closes me

in fragrance. I can
eat as I go.

We are a meadow where the bees hum,
mind and body are almost one

as the fire snaps in the stove
and our eyes close,

and mouth to mouth, the covers
pulled over our shoulders,

we drowse as horses drowse afield,
in accord; though the fall cold

surrounds our warm bed, and though
by day we are singular and often lonely.

i The Disclosure

He-who-came-forth was
it turned out
a man—

Moves among us from room to room of our life
in boots, in jeans, in a cloak of flame
pulled out of his pocket along with
old candywrappers, where it had lain
transferred from pants to pants,
folded small as a curl of dust,
from the beginning—

unfurled now.

The fine flame
almost unseen in common light.

ii The Woodblock

He cuts into a slab of wood,
engrossed, violently precise.
Thus, yesterday, the day before yesterday,
engines of fantasy were evolved
in poster paints. Tonight
a face forms under the knife,

slashed with stern
crisscrosses of longing, downstrokes
of silence endured—
                    his visioned
own face!—
down which from one eye

rolls a tear.
          His own face
drawn from the wood,

deep in the manhood his childhood
so swiftly led to, a small brook rock-leaping
into the rapt, imperious, seagoing river.

'Living a life'—
the beauty of deep lines
dug in your cheeks.

The years gather by sevens
to fashion you. They are blind,
but you are not blind.

Their blows resound,
they are deaf, those laboring
daughters of the Fates,

but you are not deaf,
you pick out
your own song from the uproar

line by line,
and at last throw back
your head and sing it.

O Eros, silently smiling one, hear me.
Let the shadow of thy wings
brush me.
Let thy presence
enfold me, as if darkness
were swandown.
Let me see that darkness
lamp in hand,
this country become
the other country
sacred to desire.

Drowsy god,
slow the wheels of my thought
so that I listen only
to the snowfall hush of
thy circling.
Close my beloved with me
in the smoke ring of thy power,
that we may be, each to the other,
figures of flame,
figures of smoke,
figures of flesh
newly seen in the dusk.

II   THE EARTH WORM

Making it, making it,
in their chosen field
the roses fall
victim to a weakness of the heart.

Scoring
        so high
no one counts the cost.
The blue moon
light on their profusion darkens.

The Earth Worm

The worm artist
out of soil, by passage
of himself
constructing.
Castles of metaphor!
Delicate
           dungeon turrets!
He throws off
artifacts as he
contracts and expands the
muscle of his being,
ringed in himself,
tilling. He
is homage to
earth, aerates
the ground of his living.

The Unknown

for Muriel Rukeyser

The kettle changes its note,
the steam sublimed.

Supererogatory divinations one is
lured on by!
                          The routine
is decent. As if the white page
were a clean tablecloth,
as if the vacuumed floor were
a primed canvas, as if
new earrings made from old shells
of tasty abalone were nose rings for the two most beautiful
girls of a meticulous island, whose bodies are oiled as one oils
a table of teak . . . Hypocrisies
of seemly hope, performed to make a place
for miracles to occur; and if the day
is no day for miracles, then the preparations
are an order one may rest in.

                          But one doesn't want
rest, one wants miracles. Each time that note
changes (which is whenever you let it)—the kettle
(already boiling) passing into enlightenment without
a moment's pause, out of fury into
quiet praise—desire
wakes again. *Begin over.*

It is to hunt a white deer
in snowy woods. Beaten
you fall asleep in the afternoon
on a sofa.

And wake to witness,
softly backing away from you, mollified,
all that the room had insisted on—
eager furniture, differentiated planes. . .
Twilight has come, the windows
are big and solemn, brimful of the afterglow;
and sleep has swept through the mind, loosening
brown leaves from their twigs to drift
out of sight
beyond the horizon's black rooftops.
A winter's dirt
makes Indian silk squares of the windowpanes,
semi transparent, a designed
middle distance.

The awakening is
to transformation,
word after word.

Brown and silver, the tufted
rushes hold sway
by the Hackensack

and small sunflowers
freckled with soot
clamber out of the fill

in gray haze of
Indian summer
among the paraphernalia

of oil refineries, the crude
industrial débris,
leftover shacks

rusting under dark
wings of Skyway—

tenacious dreamers
sifting the wind
day and night, their roots

in seeping waters—

and fierce in each disk
of coarse yellow the archaic
smile, almost
agony, almost

a boy's grin.

The flowerlike
animal perfume
in the god's curly
hair—

don't assume
that like a flower's
his attributes
are there to tempt

you or
direct the moth's
hunger—
simply he is
the temple of himself,

hair and hide
a sacrifice of blood and flowers
on his altar

if any worshipper
kneel or not.

III   THE CRUST

Joy

You must love the crust of the earth
on which you dwell. You must be
able to extract nutriment out of a
sandheap. You must have so good
an appetite as this, else you will live
in vain.

Thoreau

Joy, the, 'well . . . *joyfulness* of
joy'—'many years
I had not known it,' the woman of eighty
said, 'only remembered, till now.'

Traherne
in dark fields.
          On Tremont Street,
on the Common, a raw dusk, Emerson
'glad to the brink of fear.'
          It is objective,

stands founded, a roofed gateway;
we cloud-wander

away from it, stumble
again towards it not seeing it,

enter cast-down, discover ourselves
'in joy' as 'in love.'

33

ii

       'They knocked an
old scar off—the pent blood
rivered out and out—
          When I

white and weak, understood what befell me

speech quickened in me, I
came to myself,'
       —a poet
fifty years old, her look a pool
whose sands have down-spiralled, each grain

dream-clear now, the water
freely itself, visible transparence.

iii

Seeing the locus of joy as the gate
of a city, or as a lych-gate,

I looked up lych-gate: it means
body-gate—here the bearers

rested the bier till the priest came
(to ferry it into a new world).
                'You bring me

life!' Rilke cried to his
deathbed visitor; then, 'Help me

34

towards my death,' then, 'Never forget,
dear one, life is
magnificent!'
        I looked up 'Joy'
in *Origins,* and came to

'Jubilation' that goes back
to 'a cry of joy or woe' or to 'echoic
iu of wonder.'

iv

Again the old lady
sure for the first time there is a term
to her earth-life

enters the gate—'Joy is
so special a thing, vivid—'

her love for the earth
returns, her heart lightens,
she savors the crust.

The Willows of Massachusetts

Animal willows of November
in pelt of gold enduring when all else
has let go all ornament
and stands naked in the cold.
Cold shine of sun on swamp water,
cold caress of slant beam on bough,
gray light on brown bark.
Willows—last to relinquish a leaf,
curious, patient, lion-headed, tense
with energy, watching
the serene cold through a curtain
of tarnished strands.

Arbor vitae, whose grooved bole
reveals so many broken
intentions, branches
lopped or
wizened off,

in the grass near you
your scions are uprising,
fernlike, trustful.

Living While It May

The young elm that must be cut
because its roots push at the house wall

taps and scrapes my window
urgently—but when I look round at it

remains still. Or if I turn by chance,
it seems its leaves are eyes, or the whole spray
of leaves and twigs a face flattening
its nose against the glass, breathing a cloud,

longing to see clearly my life whose term
is not yet known.

Annuals

('Plants that flower the first season
the seed is sown, and then die')

All I planted came up,
balsam and nasturtium and
cosmos and the Marvel of Peru

first the cotyledon
then thickly the differentiated
true leaves of the seedlings,

and I transplanted them,
carefully shaking out each one's
hairfine rootlets from the earth,

and they have thriven,
well-watered in the new-turned earth;
and grow apace now—

but not one shows signs of a flower,
not one.
          If August passes
flowerless,
and the frosts come,

will I have learned to rejoice enough
in the sober wonder of
green healthy leaves?

The cat on my bosom
sleeping and purring
—fur-petalled chrysanthemum,
squirrel-killer—

is a metaphor only if I
force him to be one,
looking too long in his pale, fond,
dilating, contracting eyes

that reject mirrors, refuse
to observe what bides
stockstill.
           Likewise

flex and reflex of claws
gently pricking through sweater to skin
gently sustains their own tune,
not mine. I-Thou, cat, I-Thou.

When to my melancholy
All is folly
        then the whirr
of the hummingbird
at intervals throughout the day

is all that's sure
to stir me, makes me
jump up, scattering

papers, books, pens—
        To the bay window,
and certainly

there he is below it
true-aimed at the minute cups of
Coral Bells, swerving

perfectly,
the fierce, brilliant faith
that pierces the heart all summer

and sips bitter insects steeped in nectar,
prima materia
of gleam-and-speed-away.

A passion so intense
It driveth sorrow hence. . .

IV   THE SORROW DANCE

A headless squirrel, some blood
oozing from the unevenly
chewed-off neck

lies in rainsweet grass
near the woodshed door.
Down the driveway

the first irises
have opened since dawn,
ethereal, their mauve

almost a transparent gray,
their dark veins
bruise-blue.

Those groans men use
passing a woman on the street
or on the steps of the subway

to tell her she is a female
and their flesh knows it,

are they a sort of tune,
an ugly enough song, sung
by a bird with a slit tongue

but meant for music?

Or are they the muffled roaring
of deafmutes trapped in a building that is
slowly filling with smoke?

Perhaps both.

Such men most often
look as if groan were all they could do,
yet a woman, in spite of herself,

knows it's a tribute:
if she were lacking all grace
they'd pass her in silence:

so it's not only to say she's
a warm hole. It's a word

in grief-language, nothing to do with
primitive, not an ur-language;
language stricken, sickened, cast down

in decrepitude. She wants to
throw the tribute away, dis-
gusted, and can't,

it goes on buzzing in her ear,
it changes the pace of her walk,
the torn posters in echoing corridors

spell it out, it
quakes and gnashes as the train comes in.
Her pulse sullenly

had picked up speed,
but the cars slow down and
jar to a stop while her understanding

keeps on translating:
'Life after life after life goes by

without poetry,
without seemliness,
without love.'

In world, world
of terror,
filling up fast with
unintelligible
signs:

imploring pinkpalmed hand
twitching, autonomous,
hung from an ordinary
black arm
          (the lights change,
              it's gone)

wind
skirting the
clots of spittle,
smears of
dogshit, pushing

shadows of unknown
objects across and
away and
half across the
sidewalks, arhythmic.

The impasto of what is past,
the purple!
        Avalanches
of swarthy yellow!
              But the unremembered
makes itself into a granite-hued
nylon scarf, tight at the throat—
flies out
        backwards, a drifting
banner, tangles
the wheel.

In a landscape of boxed interiors,
among clefts, revealed strata, roofed-over
shafts, the road roves.
             A shadow

not of a bird, not of a cloud,
draws a dark stroke over
the hills, the mind.
And another, another.
Our fears keep pace with us.
We are driven.
We drive

on, shift gears, grind
up into the present in first, stop,
look out, look down.
In dust
        the lace designs incised

by feet of beetles:
paths crossing, searching—
here a broad swathe
where manna was found, and dragged
away to be savored.

                    At the horizon

flowers
vaster than cathedrals
are crowding. The motor idles.
Over the immense upland
the pulse of their blossoming
thunders through us.

At It Happens

Like dogs in Mexico,
furless, sore, misshapen,

arrives from laborious nowhere
Agony. And proves

to have eyes of kindness,
a pitiful tail; wants

love. Give it some, in form of
dry tortilla, it

grabs and runs off
three-leggéd, scared,

but tarries nearby and will
return. A friend.

Grief, have I denied thee?
Grief, I have denied thee.

That robe or tunic, black gauze
over black and silver my sister wore
to dance *Sorrow*, hung so long
in my closet. I never tried it on.
                    And my dance
was *Summer*—they rouged my cheeks
and twisted roses with wire stems into my hair.
I was compliant, Juno de sept ans,
betraying my autumn birthright pour faire plaisir.
Always denial. Grief in the morning, washed away
in coffee, crumbled to a dozen errands between
busy fingers.

              Or across cloistral shadow, insistent
intrusion of pink sunstripes from open
archways, falling recurrent.

Corrosion denied, the figures the acid designs
filled in. Grief dismissed,
and Eros along with grief.
Phantasmagoria swept across the sky
by shaky winds endlessly,
the spaces of blue timidly steady—
blue curtains at trailer windows framing
the cinder walks.
There are hidden corners of sky
choked with the swept shreds, with pain and ashes.
                                        Grief,

have I denied thee? Denied thee.
The emblems torn from the walls,
and the black plumes.

(*Olga Levertoff, 1914–1964*)

i

By the gas-fire, kneeling
to undress,
scorching luxuriously, raking
her nails over olive sides, the red
waistband ring—

(And the little sister
beady-eyed in the bed—
or drowsy, was I? My head
a camera—)

Sixteen. Her breasts
round, round, and
dark-nippled—

who now these two months long
is bones and tatters of flesh in earth.

ii

The high pitch of
nagging insistence, lines
creased into raised brows—

Ridden, ridden—
the skin around the nails
nibbled sore—

You wanted
to shout the world to its senses,
did you?—to browbeat

the poor into joy's
socialist republic—
What rage

and human shame swept you
when you were nine and saw
the Ley Street houses,

grasping their meaning as *slum*.
Where I, reaching that age,
teased you, admiring

architectural probity, circa
eighteen-fifty, and noted
pride in the whitened doorsteps.

Black one, black one,
there was a white
candle in your heart.

iii

               i

Everything flows
            she muttered into my childhood,
pacing the trampled grass where human puppets
rehearsed fates that summer,
stung into alien semblances by the lash of her will—

everything flows—
I looked up from my Littlest Bear's cane armchair
and knew the words came from a book
and felt them alien to me

but linked to words we loved
                              from the hymnbook—*Time*
like an ever-rolling stream / bears all its sons away—

                         ii

Now as if smoke or sweetness were blown my way
I inhale a sense of her livingness in that instant,
feeling, dreaming, hoping, knowing boredom and zest like anyone
                                                          else—
a young girl in the garden, the same alchemical square
I grew in, we thought sometimes
too small for our grand destinies—
                         But dread
was in her, a bloodbeat, it was against the rolling dark
oncoming river she raised bulwarks, setting herself
to sift cinders after early Mass all of one winter,

labelling her desk's normal disorder, basing
her verses on Keble's *Christian Year*, picking
those endless arguments, pressing on

to manipulate lives to disaster . . . To change,
to change the course of the river! What rage for order
disordered her pilgrimage—so that for years at a time

she would hide among strangers, waiting
to rearrange all mysteries in a new light.

iii

Black one, incubus—
　　　she appeared
riding anguish as Tartars ride mares

over the stubble of bad years.

In one of the years
　　　when I didn't know if she were dead or alive
I saw her in dream

haggard and rouged
　　　　　lit by the flare
from an eel- or cockle-stand on a slum street—

was it a dream? I had lost

all sense, almost, of
　　　who she was, what—inside of her skin,
under her black hair
　　　　　　　　dyed blonde—

it might feel like to be, in the wax and wane of the moon,
in the life I feel as unfolding, not flowing, the pilgrim years—

iv

On your hospital bed you lay
in love, the hatreds
that had followed you, a
comet's tail, burned out

as your disasters bred of love
burned out,
while pain and drugs
quarreled like sisters in you—

lay afloat on a sea
of love and pain—how you always
loved that cadence, 'Underneath
are the everlasting arms'—

all history
burned out, down
to the sick bone, save for

that kind candle.

v

i

In a garden grene whenas I lay—

you set the words to a tune so plaintive
it plucks its way through my life as through a wood.

As through a wood, shadow and light between birches,
gliding a moment in open glades, hidden by thickets of holly

your life winds in me.   In Valentines
a root protrudes from the greensward several yards from its tree

we might raise like a trapdoor's handle, you said,
and descend long steps to another country

where we would live without father or mother
and without longing for the upper world. *The birds
sang sweet,* O song, *in the midst of the daye,*

and we entered silent mid-Essex churches on hot afternoons
and communed with the effigies of knights and their ladies

and their slender dogs asleep at their feet,
the stone so cold—   *In youth*

is pleasure, in youth is pleasure.

ii

Under autumn clouds, under white
wideness of winter skies you went walking
the year you were most alone

returning to the old roads, seeing again
the signposts pointing to Theydon Garnon
or Stapleford Abbots or Greensted,

crossing the ploughlands (whose color I named *murple,*
a shade between brown and mauve that we loved
when I was a child and you

not much more than a child) finding new lanes
near White Roding or Abbess Roding; or lost in Romford's
new streets where there were footpaths then—

frowning as you ground out your thoughts, breathing deep
of the damp still air, taking
the frost into your mind unflinching.

How cold it was in your thin coat, your down-at-heel shoes—
tearless Niobe, your children were lost to you
and the stage lights had gone out, even the empty theater

was locked to you, cavern of transformation where all
had almost been possible.
                              How many books
you read in your silent lodgings that winter,
how the plovers transpierced your solitude out of doors with their
                                                    strange cries
I had flung open my arms to in longing, once, by your side
stumbling over the furrows—

Oh, in your torn stockings, with unwaved hair,
you were trudging after your anguish
over the bare fields, soberly, soberly.

vi

Your eyes were the brown gold of pebbles under water.
I never crossed the bridge over the Roding, dividing
the open field of the present from the mysteries,
the wraiths and shifts of time-sense Wanstead Park held suspended,
without remembering your eyes. Even when we were estranged
and my own eyes smarted in pain and anger at the thought of you.
And by other streams in other countries; anywhere where the light
reaches down through shallows to gold gravel. Olga's
brown eyes. One rainy summer, down in the New Forest,
when we could hardly breathe for ennui and the low sky,
you turned savagely to the piano and sightread
straight through all the Beethoven sonatas, day after day—
weeks, it seemed to me. I would turn the pages some of the time,
go out to ride my bike, return—you were enduring in the

falls and rapids of the music, the arpeggios rang out, the rectory
trembled, our parents seemed effaced.
I think of your eyes in that photo, six years before I was born,
the fear in them. What did you do with your fear,
later? Through the years of humiliation,
of paranoia and blackmail and near-starvation, losing
the love of those you loved, one after another,
parents, lovers, children, idolized friends, what kept
compassion's candle alight in you, that lit you
clear into another chapter (but the same book) 'a clearing
in the selva oscura,
a house whose door
swings open, a hand beckons
in welcome'?
           I cross
so many brooks in the world, there is so much light
dancing on so many stones, so many questions my eyes
smart to ask of your eyes, gold brown eyes,
the lashes short but the lids
arched as if carved out of olivewood, eyes with some vision
of festive goodness in back of their hard, or veiled, or shining,
unknowable gaze. . .

May–August, 1964

NOTE: The quoted lines in the sixth section are an adapta-
tion of some lines in 'Selva Oscura' by the late Louis Mac-
Neice, a poem much loved by my sister.

Ugly look, close to tears, on a man's face—
      hath compassion
      no name for it?
Look not unlike a fearful animal's
snarl as the hunter backs him up,
      but here
      no bite showing,
      the lips drawn down not back.

Drawn down, sweet lips
      of a man
as if Laurel were about
to cry—compassion
      turns in on itself
biting its tongue, unable to cry out
      or give it a name.

The Closed World

'If the Perceptive Organs close, their
Objects seem to close also.'

Blake: *Jerusalem*

The house-snake dwells here still
under the threshold
but for months I have not seen it
nor its young, the inheritors.

Light and the wind enact
passion and resurrection
day in, day out
but the blinds are down over my windows,
my doors are shut.

When after the long drought at last
silver and darkness swept over the hills
the dry indifferent glare in my mind's eye
wavered but burned on.

To speak of sorrow
works upon it
         moves it from its
crouched place barring
the way to and from the soul's hall—

out in the light it
shows clear, whether
shrunken or known as
a giant wrath—
            discrete
at least, where before

its great shadow joined
the walls and roof and seemed
to uphold the hall like a beam.

V   PERSPECTIVES

Psalm Concerning the Castle

Let me be at the place of the castle.

Let the castle be within me.

Let it rise foursquare from the moat's ring.

Let the moat's waters reflect green plumage of ducks, let the shells of swimming turtles break the surface or be seen through the rippling depths.

Let horsemen be stationed at the rim of it, and a dog, always alert on the brink of sleep.

Let the space under the first storey be dark, let the water lap the stone posts, and vivid green slime glimmer upon them; let a boat be kept there.

Let the caryatids of the second storey be bears upheld on beams that are dragons.

On the parapet of the central room, let there be four archers, looking off to the four horizons. Within, let the prince be at home, let him sit in deep thought, at peace, all the windows open to the loggias.

Let the young queen sit above, in the cool air, her child in her arms; let her look with joy at the great circle, the pilgrim shadows, the work of the sun and the play of the wind. Let her walk to and fro. Let the columns uphold the roof, let the storeys uphold the columns, let there be dark space below the lowest floor, let the castle rise foursquare out of the moat, let the moat be a ring and the water deep, let the guardians guard it, let there be wide lands around it, let that country where it stands be within me, let me be where it is.

The dawn alps,
the stilled snake of
river asleep in its
wide bed,

'to exemplify something we desire in our
own nature.'

Or six miles down
below our hawkstill swiftness

> the sea
> wakening.

And when we
come to earth the roofs
are made of tiles,
pigeons
are walking on them,

little bushes
become shade trees.

The Postcards: A Triptych

The Minoan Snake Goddess is flanked by a Chardin still-life, somber
and tranquil, and by Mohammedan angels
brilliantly clothed and with multicolored wings,
who throng round a fleshcolored horse with a man's face
on whose back rides a white-turbanned being without a face,
merely a white, oval disk, and whose hands too are unformed, or
                                                              hidden
in blue sleeves.
                    Are the angels bringing attributes
        to this unconscious one?
Is he about to be made human?
                                    One bends to the floor of heaven in
                                                              prayer;
one brings a bowl (of water?) another a tray (of food?); two
point the way, one watches from on high, two and two more
indicate measure, that is, they present
limits that confine the way to a single path;
two debate the outcome, the last
prays not bowed down but looking
level towards the pilgrim.
Stars and the winding
ceintures of the angels surround
the gold cloud or flame before which he rides; heaven itself
is a dark blue.
                    Meanwhile the still-life offers, makes possible,
a glass of water, a wine-bottle made of glass so dark it is
almost black yet not opaque, half full of
perhaps water; and besides these, two courgettes
with rough, yellow-green, almost reptilian skins,
        and a shallow basket
of plums, each almost cleft
with ripeness, the bloom upon them, their skin
darker purple or almost crimson where a hand
touched them, placing them here. Surely

this table, these fruits, these vessels, this water
stand in a cool room, stonefloored, quiet.
And the Goddess?
                              She stands
between the worlds.
                              She is ivory,
her breast bare, her bare arms
braceleted with gold snakes. Their heads
uprear towards her in homage.
Gold borders the tiers of her skirt, a gold hoop
is locked round her waist. She is a few inches high.
And she muses, her lips are pursed,
beneath her crown that must once have been studded with gold
she frowns, she gazes
at and beyond her snakes as if
not goddess but priestess, waiting
an augury.
                    Without thought I have placed these images
over my desk. Under these signs
I am living.

How I woke to the color-tone
as of peach-juice
dulcet bells were
tolling.
       And how my pleasure
was in the strength of my back,
in my noble shoulders, the cool
smooth flesh cylinders of my arms.
How I seemed a woman tall and
full-rounded, ready
to step into daylight sound as a bell

but continued to awake
further, and found myself
myself, smaller,
not thin but thinner, nervous,
who hurries without animal calm.
And how the sweet
blur of the bells

lapsed, and ceased,
and it was not morning.

City Psalm

The killings continue, each second
pain and misfortune extend themselves
in the genetic chain, injustice is done knowingly, and the air
bears the dust of decayed hopes,
yet breathing those fumes, walking the thronged
pavements among crippled lives, jackhammers
raging, a parking lot painfully agleam
in the May sun, I have seen
not behind but within, within the
dull grief, blown grit, hideous
concrete façades, another grief, a gleam
as of dew, an abode of mercy,
have heard not behind but within noise
a humming that drifted into a quiet smile.
Nothing was changed, all was revealed otherwise;
not that horror was not, not that the killings did not continue,
not that I thought there was to be no more despair,
but that as if transparent all disclosed
an otherness that was blesséd, that was bliss.
I saw Paradise in the dust of the street.

A Vision

'The intellectual love of a thing is
the understanding of its perfections.'
Spinoza, quoted by Ezra Pound

Two angels among the throng of angels
paused in the upward abyss,
facing angel to angel.

Blue and green glowed the wingfeathers
of one angel, from red to gold the sheen
of the other's. These two,

so far as angels may dispute, were poised
on the brink of dispute, brink of
fall from angelic stature,

for these tall ones, angels
whose wingspan encompasses entire
earthly villages, whose heads if their feet touched earth

would top pines or redwoods, live by their vision's harmony
which sees at one glance
the dark and light of the moon.

These two hovered dazed before one another,
for one saw the seafeathered, peacock breakered
crests of the other angel's magnificence,
different from his own,

and the other's eyes flickered with vision of
flame petallings, cream-gold grainfeather glitterings,
the wings of his fellow,

73

and both in immortal danger of dwindling, of dropping
into the remote forms of a lesser being.

But as these angels, the only halted ones
among the many who passed and repassed,
trod air as swimmers tread water, each gazing

on the angelic wings of the other,
the intelligence proper to great angels flew into their wings,
the intelligence called *intellectual love,* which,
understanding the perfections of scarlet,

leapt up among blues and green strongshafted,
and among amber down illumined the sapphire bloom,

so that each angel was iridescent with the strange newly-seen
hues he watched; and their discovering pause
and the speech their silent interchange of perfection was

never became a shrinking to opposites,

and they remained free in the heavenly chasm,
remained angels, but dreaming angels,
each imbued with the mysteries of the other.

VI   LIFE AT WAR

The Pulse

Sealed inside the anemone
in the dark, I knock my head
on steel petals
curving inward around me.

Somewhere the edict is given:
petals, relax.
Delicately they arch over backward.
All is opened to me—

the air they call *water,*
saline, dawngreen over its sands,
resplendent with fishes.
All day it is morning,

all night the glitter
of all that shines out of itself
crisps the vast swathes of the current.
But my feet are weighted:

only my seafern arms
my human hands
my fingers tipped with fire
sway out into the world.

Fair is the world.
I sing. The ache
up from heel to knee
of the weights

gives to the song its
ground bass.
And before the song
attains even a first refrain

the petals creak and
begin to rise.
They rise and recurl
to a bud's form

and clamp shut.
I wait in the dark.

The disasters numb within us
caught in the chest, rolling
in the brain like pebbles. The feeling
resembles lumps of raw dough

weighing down a child's stomach on baking day.
Or Rilke said it, 'My heart. . .
Could I say of it, it overflows
with bitterness . . . but no, as though

its contents were simply balled into
formless lumps, thus
do I carry it about.'
The same war

continues.
We have breathed the grits of it in, all our lives,
our lungs are pocked with it,
the mucous membrane of our dreams
coated with it, the imagination
filmed over with the gray filth of it:

the knowledge that humankind,

delicate Man, whose flesh
responds to a caress, whose eyes
are flowers that perceive the stars,

whose music excels the music of birds,
whose laughter matches the laughter of dogs,
whose understanding manifests designs
fairer than the spider's most intricate web,

still turns without surprise, with mere regret
to the scheduled breaking open of breasts whose milk
runs out over the entrails of still-alive babies,
transformation of witnessing eyes to pulp-fragments,
implosion of skinned penises into carcass-gulleys.

We are the humans, men who can make;
whose language imagines *mercy,*
lovingkindness; we have believed one another
mirrored forms of a God we felt as good—

who do these acts, who convince ourselves
it is necessary; these acts are done
to our own flesh; burned human flesh
is smelling in Viet Nam as I write.

Yes, this is the knowledge that jostles for space
in our bodies along with all we
go on knowing of joy, of love;

our nerve filaments twitch with its presence
day and night,
nothing we say has not the husky phlegm of it in the saying,
nothing we do has the quickness, the sureness,
the deep intelligence living at peace would have.

Didactic Poem

The blood we give the dead to drink
is deeds we do at the will of the dead spirits in us,
not our own live will.
The dead who thirst to speak
had no good of words or deeds when they lived,
or not enough, and were left in longing.
Their longing to speak, their thirst
for the blood of their deeds done by us,
would leave no time, place, force,
for our own deeds, our own
imagination of speech.
Refuse them!
If we too miss out, don't create our lives,
                  invent our deeds, do them, dance
                  a tune with our own feet,
we shall thirst in Hades,
in the blood of our children.

The honey of man is
the task we're set to: to be
'more ourselves'
in the making:
                'bees of the invisible' working
in cells of flesh and psyche,
filling
      'la grande ruche d'or.'

Nectar,
       the makings of the
incorruptible,
           is carried upon the
corrupt tongues of
mortal insects,
fanned with their wisps of wing
           'to evaporate
excess water,'
         enclosed and capped
with wax, the excretion
of bees' abdominal glands.
Beespittle, droppings, hairs
of beefur: all become honey.
Virulent micro-organisms cannot
survive in honey.
         The taste,
the odor of honey:
each has no analogue but itself.

In our gathering, in our containing, in our
working, active within ourselves,
slowly the pale
dew-beads of light
lapped up from flowers
can thicken,
darken to gold:

honey of the human.

1) Did the people of Viet Nam
   use lanterns of stone?
2) Did they hold ceremonies
   to reverence the opening of buds?
3) Were they inclined to quiet laughter?
4) Did they use bone and ivory,
   jade and silver, for ornament?
5) Had they an epic poem?
6) Did they distinguish between speech and singing?

1) Sir, their light hearts turned to stone.
   It is not remembered whether in gardens
   stone lanterns illumined pleasant ways.
2) Perhaps they gathered once to delight in blossom,
   but after the children were killed
   there were no more buds.
3) Sir, laughter is bitter to the burned mouth.
4) A dream ago, perhaps. Ornament is for joy.
   All the bones were charred.
5) It is not remembered. Remember,
   most were peasants; their life
   was in rice and bamboo.
   When peaceful clouds were reflected in the paddies
   and the water buffalo stepped surely along terraces,
   maybe fathers told their sons old tales.
   When bombs smashed those mirrors
   there was time only to scream.
6) There is no echo yet
   of their speech which was like a song.
   It was reported their singing resembled
   the flight of moths in moonlight.
   Who can say? It is silent now.

Two Variations

i Enquiry

You who go out on schedule
to kill, do you know
there are eyes that watch you,
eyes whose lids you burned off,
that see you eat your steak
and buy your girlflesh
and sell your PX goods
and sleep?
She is not old,
she whose eyes
know you.
She will outlast you.
She saw
her five young children
writhe and die;
in that hour
she began to watch you,
she whose eyes are open forever.

ii The Seeing

Hands over my eyes I see
blood and the little bones;
or when a blanket covers
the sockets I see the
weave; at night the glare softens
but I have power now
to see there is only gray
on gray, the sleepers, the
altar. I see the living
and the dead; the dead are

as if alive, the mouth of
my youngest son pulls my
breast, but there is no milk, he
is a ghost; through his flesh
I see the dying of those
said to be alive, they
eat rice and speak to me but
I see dull death in them
and while they speak I see
myself on my mat, body
and eyes, eyes that see a
hand in the unclouded sky,
a human hand, release
wet fire, the rain that gave
my eyes their vigilance.

The Altars in the Street

On June 17th, 1966, The New York Times
reported that, as part of the Buddhist cam-
paign of passive non-resistance, Viet-Namese
children were building altars in the streets
of Saigon and Hue, effectively jamming
traffic.

Children begin at green dawn nimbly to build
topheavy altars, overweighted with prayers,
thronged each instant more densely

with almost-visible ancestors.
Where tanks have cracked the roadway
the frail altars shake; here a boy

with red stumps for hands steadies a corner,
here one adjusts with his crutch the holy base.
The vast silence of Buddha overtakes

and overrules the oncoming roar
of tragic life that fills alleys and avenues;
it blocks the way of pedicabs, police, convoys.

The hale and maimed together
hurry to construct for the Buddha
a dwelling at each intersection. Each altar

made from whatever stones, sticks, dreams, are at hand,
is a facet of one altar; by noon
the whole city in all its corruption,

all its shed blood the monsoon cannot wash away,
has become a temple,
fragile, insolent, absolute.

i

Of lead and emerald
the reliquary
that knocks my breastbone,

slung round my neck
on a rough invisible rope
that rubs the knob of my spine.

Though I forget you
a red coal from your fire
burns in that box.

ii

On the Times Square sidewalk
we shuffle along, cardboard signs
—Stop the War—
slung round our necks.

The cops
hurry about,
shoulder to shoulder,
comic.

Your high soprano
sings out from just
in back of me—

We shall—I turn,
you're, I very well know,
not there,

and your voice, they say,
grew hoarse
from shouting at crowds. . .

yet *overcome*
sounds then hoarsely
from somewhere in front,

the paddywagon
gapes. —It seems
you that is lifted

limp and ardent
off the dark snow
and shoved in, and driven away.

The fire in leaf and grass
so green it seems
each summer the last summer.

The wind blowing, the leaves
shivering in the sun,
each day the last day.

A red salamander
so cold and so
easy to catch, dreamily

moves his delicate feet
and long tail. I hold
my hand open for him to go.

Each minute the last minute.

VII   A POEM BY OLGA LEVERTOFF

The Ballad of My Father

'Yáchchiderálum, pútzele mútzele:
    why is your fóotzele burnt to the bone?'
'Hail, dear Rabboni! We would not leave you lonely!
    We come from the limepit where millions were
        thrown!'

My father danced a Hassidic dance the day before he died.
His daughters they were far away, his wife was by his side.

'Yes, from concentration camps, and yes, from gas chambers:
    from thousand years' ghettos, from graves old and new—
Our unremembered bones come to caper in your
        drawingroom,
    and join in the death-dance of one holy Jew!'

He danced for Jesus his Messiah who rose up from the dead
And left the tomb for the upper room and was known
        in the breaking of bread.

'Those who were faithful, and those who betrayed them,
    those who did nothing, and those who defied—
Here they come crowding—the grave has but delayed them:
    your people surround you, in shame and in pride.'

Except you become as a little child my kingdom
        you shall not see.
So he danced in his joy as he did when a boy
        and as often he danced for me.

'Yáchchiderálum, pútzele mútzele:
    faster and faster the measure we tread!
Your hand in my hand, your foot to my footzele—
    partners for ever, the living and the dead!'

He danced for those he left long ago and for those
　　　　he never knew,
For an end of strife for eternal life for behold
　　　　I make all things new.

'Come, tread the winepress! The blood of the ages
　　　　squeezed from our flesh shall be our loving cup:
Red river of life, drawn from martyrs and sages,
　　　　shall bear you on its tide till your Lord
　　　　shall raise you up!'

My father danced a Hassidic dance and sang
　　　　with his latest breath
The dance of peace it will never cease till life
　　　　has conquered death.

'Yáchchiderálum, pútzele mútzele—
　　　　who will remember and who will forget?'
Twirling down time's corridors I see your shadow dancing—
　　　　your song echoes clear down the years whose
　　　　sun has set.

My father danced and then he died and his name
　　　　is a long time gone.
His voice was stilled and his task fulfilled for a people
　　　　that shall be born.

Yáchchiderálum, pútzele mútzele—
　　　　now if I couldzele I'd speak to you true:
But your dance it is ended and all the tears expended—
　　　　so sleep on and take your rest, my father, my Jew.

　　　　　　　　　　　　　Olga Levertoff
November, 1963

94